Table Of Contents

The Importance of Financial Literacy 2
The Impact of Financial Literacy on Personal Finances 2
Common Financial Mistakes and How to Avoid Them 2
Chapter 2: Assessing Your Current Financial Situation.......................2
Evaluating Income and Expenses 2
Tracking and Analyzing Spending Habits..2
Understanding Your Debt and Credit Score......................................2
Assessing Your Assets and Liabilities 2
Chapter 3: Setting Financial Goals..2
Identifying Short-term and Long-term Financial Goals..................2
Creating a Realistic Budget...2
Saving and Investing for the Future 2
The Power of Compound Interest 2
Chapter 4: Building Healthy Financial Habits.......................................2
Developing a Savings Mindset 2
Smart Spending Strategies 2
Automating Bill Payments and Savings..2
Establishing an Emergency Fund..2
Chapter 5: Improving Time Management for Financial Success 2
Prioritizing Financial Tasks 2
Creating a Daily and Weekly Financial Routine...............................2
Using Technology for Efficient Money Management 2
Delegating and Outsourcing Financial Responsibilities.................2
Chapter 6: Organizing Your Financial Life 2
Setting Up a Filing System for Financial Documents......................2
Managing Digital Financial Records..2

Simplifying and Optimizing Financial Accounts 2
Reviewing and Updating Insurance Policies......................................2
Chapter 7: Overcoming Fear and Phobias Related to Finances 2
Identifying and Addressing Money Anxiety......................................2
Confronting Financial Phobias and Overcoming Them 2
Seeking Professional Help and Support 2
Building Confidence in Financial Decision-Making..........................2
Chapter 8: Navigating the World of Investments 2
Understanding Different Investment Options 2
Diversifying Your Investment Portfolio 2
Evaluating Risk and Return...2
Working with Financial Advisors and Investment Professionals ...2
Chapter 9: Planning for Retirement and Long-Term Financial
Security 2
Assessing Retirement Needs and Goals 2
Exploring Retirement Account Options 2
Strategies for Maximizing Social Security Benefits.........................2
Estate Planning and Wealth Transfer...2
Chapter 10: Protecting Your Financial Future 2
Understanding Insurance Coverage...2
Safeguarding Against Identity Theft and Fraud 2
Creating a Financial Safety Net 2
Continual Learning and Staying Up-to-Date with Financial Trends
....2
Chapter 11: Sustaining Financial Freedom......................................2
Reviewing and Revising Financial Goals..2
Celebrating Milestones and Progress 2
Teaching Financial Literacy to Others 2
Giving Back and Contributing to Financial Education Initiatives ...2
Chapter 1: Understanding Financial Literacy.......................................1

Chapter 1: Understanding Financial Literacy

The Importance of Financial Literacy

In today's fast-paced and ever-changing world, financial literacy has become an essential life skill. Yet, many adults struggle to understand and manage their finances effectively. The consequences of this lack of knowledge can be detrimental, leading to debt, financial stress, and missed opportunities. In this subchapter, we will delve into the importance of financial literacy and why it should be a priority for every adult.

First and foremost, financial literacy empowers individuals to make informed decisions about their money. Understanding concepts such as budgeting, saving, investing, and debt management allows individuals to take control of their financial future. With this knowledge, they can create a solid foundation for financial stability and build wealth over time.

Moreover, financial literacy plays a crucial role in building healthy habits and routines. By developing good financial habits, individuals can create a positive feedback loop that reinforces discipline, responsibility, and long-term thinking. These habits extend beyond money management and spill over into other areas of life, such as time management and organization skills. Financially literate individuals tend to be more organized, goal-oriented, and efficient, which ultimately leads to improved overall well-being.

Overcoming fear and phobias related to money is another benefit of financial literacy. Many people experience anxiety and fear when it comes to dealing with finances due to a lack of understanding. However, by acquiring financial knowledge, individuals can conquer these fears and gain confidence in their ability to handle money matters. This newfound confidence allows them to explore opportunities, take calculated risks, and pursue financial freedom with a sense of assurance.

Finally, improving financial literacy and managing money effectively can have a profound impact on an individual's quality of life. It can reduce stress, improve relationships, and provide a sense of security and freedom. Financially literate individuals are better equipped to navigate unexpected financial challenges, seize opportunities for growth, and achieve their long-term goals.

In conclusion, financial literacy is not just a nice-to-have skill; it is a necessity in today's world. It impacts various aspects of our lives, including our habits, fears, and overall well-being. By prioritizing financial literacy, adults can take control of their finances, build healthy habits, overcome fears, and ultimately improve their overall financial situation. Whether you are just starting to learn about managing money or looking to enhance your existing knowledge, this book aims to provide you with a step-by-step guide to improving financial literacy and achieving financial freedom.

The Impact of Financial Literacy on Personal Finances

In today's fast-paced and ever-changing world, it is crucial for adults to possess a strong foundation in financial literacy. The ability to understand and manage personal finances has a profound impact on our overall well-being and can significantly improve our quality of life. In this subchapter, we will explore the various ways in which financial literacy directly influences our personal finances.

One of the most significant impacts of financial literacy is the ability to make informed financial decisions. When we understand the concepts of budgeting, saving, investing, and debt management, we can make smarter choices about our money. Financially literate individuals are more likely to create and stick to a budget, avoid unnecessary debt, and make wise investment decisions that can lead to long-term financial success.

Moreover, being financially literate helps individuals develop a healthier relationship with money. Many people struggle with financial stress and anxiety due to a lack of understanding about their own financial situation. By increasing our financial literacy, we can gain a sense of control over our money and reduce the stress associated with financial uncertainty. This, in turn, allows us to focus more on our personal growth and overall well-being.

Financial literacy also plays a crucial role in achieving long-term financial goals. Whether it's saving for retirement, buying a home, or starting a business, having a solid understanding of personal finance is essential. By learning about investment strategies, risk management, and the power of compound interest, individuals can develop effective financial plans to reach their goals. Financially literate individuals are more likely to accumulate wealth, build assets, and secure their financial future.

Lastly, financial literacy empowers individuals to navigate the complex financial landscape and avoid scams and fraudulent schemes. With the rise of online financial transactions, it is increasingly important to be able to recognize and protect ourselves from financial fraud. By understanding the basics of personal finance, we can make informed decisions, protect our assets, and avoid falling victim to scams that can devastate our financial well-being.

In conclusion, financial literacy has a profound impact on our personal finances. It allows us to make informed decisions, develop a healthier relationship with money, achieve long-term financial goals, and protect ourselves from financial fraud. By investing time and effort in improving our financial literacy, we can take control of our finances and pave the way towards financial freedom and a brighter future.

Common Financial Mistakes and How to Avoid Them

In our journey towards financial freedom, it is crucial to be aware of the common financial mistakes that many individuals make. By learning from these mistakes, we can make informed decisions and take steps towards improving our financial literacy and managing money effectively. In this subchapter, we will discuss some of the most common financial mistakes and provide practical tips on how to avoid them.

One of the most prevalent mistakes people make is living beyond their means. It is easy to fall into the trap of overspending and accumulating debt. To avoid this, it is essential to create a realistic budget that aligns with your income and expenses. Track your spending and identify areas where you can cut back. Practice delayed gratification and prioritize needs over wants.

Another mistake is not having an emergency fund. Life is unpredictable, and unexpected expenses can arise at any time. By setting aside a portion of your income regularly, you can build an emergency fund that will act as a safety net during challenging times. Aim to save at least three to six months' worth of living expenses to ensure financial stability.

Investing without proper knowledge is also a common mistake. Before diving into the world of investing, take the time to educate yourself. Understand the different investment options available, assess your risk tolerance, and seek guidance from financial advisors if needed. Diversify your investment portfolio to minimize risk and maximize potential returns.

Neglecting retirement planning is another significant financial mistake. Start planning for retirement as early as possible, even if it seems far away. Explore options such as 401(k) plans, Individual Retirement Accounts (IRAs), and other retirement savings vehicles. Take advantage of employer-matching contributions and contribute consistently to achieve long-term financial security.

Lastly, failing to prioritize debt repayment can hinder your financial progress. High-interest debts, such as credit card debts, can accumulate quickly and become overwhelming. Develop a debt repayment plan, focusing on paying off high-interest debts first. Consider consolidating debts or negotiating lower interest rates to expedite the repayment process.

By avoiding these common financial mistakes, you can pave the way towards financial freedom. Take control of your finances, educate yourself, and make informed decisions. Remember, financial literacy is a lifelong journey, and by continually improving your financial habits and routines, managing time effectively, overcoming fear and phobias, and strengthening your financial literacy, you can achieve your goals and live a financially secure life.

Chapter 2: Assessing Your Current Financial Situation

Evaluating Income and Expenses

In today's fast-paced world, it can be challenging to maintain control over our finances. We often find ourselves caught up in the whirlwind of daily expenses, without a clear understanding of where our money is going. However, learning to evaluate our income and expenses is a crucial step towards achieving financial freedom. In this subchapter, we will delve into the importance of this process and provide you with practical tips to improve your financial literacy and money management skills.

Understanding your income is the first step towards building a solid financial foundation. Take the time to evaluate all sources of income, including your salary, investments, and any additional streams of revenue. By having a clear picture of your total income, you can make informed decisions about how to allocate your money effectively.

Next, it is essential to analyze your expenses. Start by categorizing them into fixed and variable expenses. Fixed expenses include bills, rent or mortgage payments, and insurance premiums. Variable expenses, on the other hand, fluctuate from month to month, such as groceries, dining out, and entertainment. By understanding the breakdown of your expenses, you can identify areas where you can make adjustments and potentially save money.

One of the most effective tools for evaluating income and expenses is creating a budget. A budget allows you to track your income and expenses, enabling you to prioritize your spending and save for future goals. When creating a budget, consider setting aside funds for emergencies, savings, and investments. This will help you build a safety net and work towards long-term financial stability.

Additionally, it is crucial to regularly review your financial situation. Set aside time each month to assess your income and expenses, ensuring that you are staying on track with your budget and financial goals. By keeping a close eye on your finances, you can make necessary adjustments and avoid any potential financial pitfalls.

Evaluating income and expenses is a fundamental step towards achieving financial freedom. By understanding your income sources, analyzing your expenses, and creating a budget, you can take control of your finances and work towards a brighter financial future. In the following chapters, we will delve deeper into various strategies for improving financial literacy and managing money effectively. Stay tuned for more valuable insights on your journey to financial freedom.

Tracking and Analyzing Spending Habits

One of the key aspects of achieving financial freedom is having a clear understanding of your spending habits. Tracking and analyzing your expenses is a crucial step towards improving your financial literacy and managing your money effectively. In this subchapter, we will explore various strategies and tools that can help you gain control over your spending habits.

To begin with, let's discuss the importance of tracking your expenses. Many individuals are unaware of how much they are spending and where their money is going. By diligently tracking your expenses, you will be able to identify patterns, cut down on unnecessary expenses, and allocate your money towards more meaningful goals. This process will empower you to take control of your financial situation and make informed decisions about your spending.

There are several methods you can use to track your expenses. One simple approach is to maintain a spending journal or use a budgeting app. These tools allow you to record your daily expenses and categorize them accordingly. By reviewing your spending patterns regularly, you can identify areas where you may be overspending and make necessary adjustments.

Analyzing your spending habits goes beyond just tracking your expenses. It involves a deeper understanding of your financial goals, values, and priorities. By aligning your spending with your long-term objectives, you can make conscious choices that reflect your values and help you reach financial independence.

Another useful strategy is to set a spending limit for different categories, such as groceries, entertainment, and transportation. This will help you stay within your budget and avoid unnecessary impulse purchases. Additionally, consider conducting a monthly or quarterly review of your spending to evaluate your progress and identify any areas that need improvement.

Furthermore, technology has made it easier than ever to analyze your spending habits. Numerous financial management apps provide detailed reports and visualizations of your expenses, making it easier to identify trends and areas for improvement. These tools can also help you set financial goals, create budgets, and track your progress towards achieving them.

In conclusion, tracking and analyzing your spending habits is a crucial step towards financial freedom. By understanding where your money is going, you can make informed decisions, cut down on unnecessary expenses, and work towards your long-term financial goals. By implementing the strategies discussed in this subchapter, you will be well on your way to improving your financial literacy and managing your money effectively.

Understanding Your Debt and Credit Score

In today's fast-paced world, it is crucial to have a clear understanding of your debt and credit score. Whether you are striving for financial freedom, building healthy habits and routines, improving time management and organization skills, or overcoming fear and phobias, having a solid grasp on your debt and credit score plays a vital role in achieving your goals.

Debt can be both a burden and a tool. It is essential to differentiate between good debt and bad debt. Good debt is an investment in your future, such as student loans or a mortgage, while bad debt includes high-interest credit cards or payday loans. Understanding the difference allows you to make informed decisions about taking on debt and managing it effectively.

To gain a comprehensive understanding of your financial situation, it is crucial to assess your credit score. Your credit score is a numerical representation of your creditworthiness and is used by lenders to determine your borrowing capacity. A good credit score opens doors to better interest rates, loan approvals, and overall financial flexibility.

Improving your credit score starts with establishing healthy financial habits. Start by reviewing your credit report for any errors or discrepancies and rectify them immediately. Create a budget that allows you to manage your expenses and pay bills on time. Aim to keep your credit utilization ratio low by using less than 30% of your available credit. Utilize credit responsibly by making regular payments and avoiding unnecessary debt.

Managing your debt is a crucial step towards achieving financial freedom. Start by organizing your debts, listing them in order of interest rates and prioritizing payment. Consider debt consolidation or negotiation strategies to lower interest rates and create a manageable repayment plan. It is essential to communicate with your creditors and seek professional advice if needed.

Understanding your debt and credit score empowers you to make informed choices about your financial future. It allows you to take control of your finances, reduce stress, and build a foundation for prosperity. The path to financial freedom begins with self-awareness, responsibility, and a commitment to improving your financial literacy and managing your money effectively.

In the following chapters, we will delve deeper into specific strategies and techniques for building healthy financial habits, improving time management and organization skills, and overcoming fear and phobias related to managing money. By combining these self-help principles with a solid understanding of your debt and credit score, you will be well on your way to achieving your financial goals and living a life of abundance.

Assessing Your Assets and Liabilities

In order to achieve financial freedom, it is crucial to have a clear understanding of your assets and liabilities. This subchapter aims to guide you through the process of assessing your financial situation, helping you gain control over your money and make informed decisions.

Firstly, let's define assets and liabilities. Assets refer to anything you own that holds value, such as cash, investments, real estate, or even your skills and knowledge. On the other hand, liabilities are your debts or financial obligations, including loans, mortgages, credit card debt, or any other outstanding payments.

To begin the assessment, start by listing all your assets. Include your bank accounts, investments, properties, vehicles, and any other valuable possessions. Don't forget to also consider your skills and expertise, as they can be monetized in various ways.

Next, turn your attention to your liabilities. List all your debts and financial obligations, including the amounts owed, interest rates, and repayment terms. This will give you a clear overview of your financial commitments.

Once you have compiled these lists, it's time to analyze your financial situation. Calculate your net worth by subtracting your liabilities from your assets. This will provide you with an accurate snapshot of your current financial standing.

Understanding your net worth is essential as it helps you identify areas of improvement and set realistic financial goals. It also allows you to track your progress over time.

In addition to assessing your net worth, it is crucial to evaluate your cash flow. Take a close look at your income and expenses, including fixed expenses (rent, utilities), variable expenses (entertainment, groceries), and discretionary spending (eating out, shopping). This analysis will help you identify areas where you can reduce expenses or increase your income.

Regularly assessing your assets and liabilities is essential for maintaining financial health. It enables you to make informed decisions about investments, debt management, and budgeting. By understanding your financial position, you can create a solid foundation for achieving financial freedom.

Remember, improving your financial literacy and managing money requires consistent effort and dedication. By taking the time to assess your assets and liabilities, you are taking a significant step towards building a secure financial future.

Chapter 3: Setting Financial Goals

Identifying Short-term and Long-term Financial Goals

In the journey towards financial freedom, it is essential to have a clear understanding of your short-term and long-term financial goals. These goals act as a compass, guiding your decision-making process and helping you stay focused on achieving financial success.

Short-term financial goals typically span a period of one year or less. They are the stepping stones towards your long-term objectives and help you build a solid foundation for your financial future. Examples of short-term goals may include creating an emergency fund, paying off credit card debt, or saving for a vacation.

Long-term financial goals, on the other hand, are usually set for a period of five years or more. These goals are more substantial and often require careful planning and diligent effort. Examples of long-term goals may include buying a home, saving for retirement, or starting your own business.

To identify your short-term and long-term financial goals, start by assessing your current financial situation. Take a comprehensive look at your income, expenses, debts, and assets. This evaluation will give you a clear picture of where you stand financially and help you determine what goals are realistic and attainable.

Next, consider your values, aspirations, and priorities. What are the things that truly matter to you? Do you dream of traveling the world, owning a luxurious car, or sending your children to college debt-free? Reflecting on these desires will help you identify meaningful and motivating financial goals.

Once you have identified your goals, it is crucial to set specific, measurable, achievable, relevant, and time-bound (SMART) objectives. Instead of saying, "I want to save money," specify how much you want to save within a specific timeframe. For example, "I want to save $10,000 for a down payment on a house in the next two years."

Regularly review and update your goals to ensure they remain relevant and aligned with your evolving financial situation and aspirations. Celebrate your achievements along the way, as this will keep you motivated and on track.

Remember, identifying short-term and long-term financial goals is just the beginning. The next steps involve creating a detailed plan, developing healthy financial habits, and implementing effective money management strategies. By doing so, you can pave the way towards financial freedom and enjoy a more secure and prosperous future.

Creating a Realistic Budget

Financial Freedom Blueprint: A Step-by-Step Guide to Improving Financial Literacy and Managing Money

Introduction:

In today's fast-paced world, it is essential to have a realistic budget that aligns with your financial goals. A well-planned budget not only helps you manage your money effectively but also provides you with a sense of control and security. In this subchapter, we will explore the step-by-step process of creating a realistic budget that empowers you to take charge of your finances and achieve financial freedom.

Step 1: Assess Your Current Financial Situation

Before creating a budget, it is important to understand where you currently stand financially. Take a comprehensive look at your income, expenses, debts, and savings. This assessment will help you identify areas that need improvement and set realistic financial goals.

Step 2: Analyze Your Spending Habits

To create an effective budget, it is crucial to examine your spending habits. Track your expenses for a few months and categorize them. Identify areas where you can cut back, such as unnecessary subscriptions or impulsive purchases. By understanding your spending patterns, you can make informed decisions and allocate your resources wisely.

Step 3: Set Realistic Financial Goals

Once you have a clear understanding of your financial situation, it's time to set realistic goals. Whether it's paying off debt, saving for retirement, or buying a house, define your goals and assign a timeline to achieve them. These goals will serve as a compass for your budget and motivate you to stick to it.

Step 4: Create a Budget Plan

Now comes the crucial step of actually crafting your budget plan. Start by allocating a portion of your income towards necessities, such as rent, utilities, groceries, and transportation. Then, determine how much you can save or invest and allocate funds accordingly. Finally, set aside a reasonable amount for discretionary expenses, such as entertainment or dining out.

Step 5: Review and Adjust

A budget is not a set-it-and-forget-it tool. Regularly review your budget to ensure you are on track. Analyze your expenses, income, and savings regularly and make adjustments as needed. Life circumstances change, and your budget should be flexible enough to accommodate those changes.

Conclusion:

Creating a realistic budget is a fundamental step towards achieving financial freedom. By assessing your current financial situation, analyzing your spending habits, setting realistic goals, and creating a budget plan, you can take control of your finances. Remember, it is essential to review and adjust your budget regularly to stay on track. With a realistic budget in place, you can build healthy financial habits, improve time management and organization skills, overcome fear and phobias related to money, and ultimately achieve financial literacy and success.

Saving and Investing for the Future

Saving and investing for the future is a crucial aspect of building financial security and ensuring a comfortable life for yourself and your loved ones. In this subchapter, we will delve into the importance of saving and investing, as well as provide practical tips and strategies to help you achieve your financial goals.

Saving for the future allows you to create a safety net for unexpected expenses and emergencies. It provides you with the peace of mind that you can handle any financial setback that may come your way. By setting aside a portion of your income regularly, you are establishing a foundation for a secure financial future.

Investing, on the other hand, allows your money to grow and work for you. While saving is important, investing allows you to beat inflation and potentially earn higher returns. It is a way of putting your money to work and making it grow over time.

To start saving and investing for the future, it is crucial to establish a budget. Knowing where your money is going and making conscious decisions about your spending habits is the first step towards financial freedom. By tracking your expenses and setting financial goals, you can identify areas where you can cut back and save more.

Another important aspect of saving and investing is understanding the power of compounding. By investing early and consistently, you can benefit from the compounding effect, which allows your money to grow exponentially over time. This means that the earlier you start investing, the more time your investments have to grow and accumulate wealth.

Diversification is also a key principle in investing. By spreading your investments across different asset classes such as stocks, bonds, and real estate, you can reduce risk and increase the potential for higher returns. Diversification helps protect your investments from market fluctuations and ensures that your portfolio is well-balanced.

In conclusion, saving and investing for the future is essential for achieving financial security and independence. By developing healthy saving habits, creating a budget, and investing wisely, you can build wealth and secure a prosperous future. Remember, it is never too early or too late to start saving and investing – the key is to take the first step and commit to a financially healthy future.

The Power of Compound Interest

In the world of finance, there is a concept that holds incredible power – compound interest. This simple yet potent force has the potential to drastically transform your financial situation if understood and utilized effectively. In this subchapter, we will delve into the intricacies of compound interest and explore how it can be harnessed to improve your financial literacy and manage your money more efficiently.

Compound interest is the phenomenon where the interest earned on an investment or debt is added to the principal amount, resulting in the interest being calculated on a larger base in the following periods. This compounding effect can create a snowball effect that accelerates the growth of your investments or the accumulation of debt.

Understanding compound interest allows you to make informed decisions about saving and investing. By starting early and consistently contributing to your investments, you can take advantage of the compounding effect over time. The longer your money remains invested, the greater the growth potential. This knowledge empowers you to establish healthy financial habits and routines, building a solid foundation for your future.

Furthermore, compound interest can aid in improving your time management and organization skills. By automating your savings and investments, you can free up mental space and time, as you won't need to constantly monitor and adjust your finances. Instead, you can focus on other areas of your life and pursue personal growth, overcoming any fears or phobias that may hinder your progress.

Financial literacy is a critical aspect of managing money effectively, and compound interest plays a fundamental role in this realm. By understanding how compound interest works, you can make informed decisions about borrowing, investing, and saving. This knowledge empowers you to take control of your financial future, enabling you to make wise choices and avoid common pitfalls.

In conclusion, the power of compound interest cannot be understated. This force has the potential to transform your financial life and provide you with the freedom and security you desire. By developing healthy habits, improving time management and organization skills, overcoming fears, and enhancing your financial literacy, you can harness the power of compound interest to build a brighter future. So, embrace this concept, educate yourself, and take action to improve your financial situation today.

Chapter 4: Building Healthy Financial Habits

Developing a Savings Mindset

In today's fast-paced and consumer-driven society, developing a savings mindset is more important than ever. It is the foundation of financial stability and a key component of achieving long-term financial freedom. In this subchapter, we will explore the importance of cultivating a savings mindset and provide practical strategies to help you develop this essential habit.

Building healthy habits and routines are crucial for success in any aspect of life, and managing money is no exception. By developing a savings mindset, you can create a routine that prioritizes saving and allows you to achieve your financial goals. This subchapter will guide you through the process of setting clear savings goals, creating a budget, and incorporating saving strategies into your daily routines.

Improving time management and organization skills go hand in hand with developing a savings mindset. By effectively managing your time, you can allocate dedicated periods for reviewing your finances, tracking your expenses, and planning your savings. This subchapter will provide practical tips on how to optimize your time, streamline your financial tasks, and ensure that saving becomes a priority in your daily schedule.

Overcoming fear and phobias around money is often a significant hurdle for many individuals. This subchapter will delve into the psychological aspects of saving and explore strategies to overcome the fear of scarcity or the belief that saving means deprivation. By addressing these fears head-on, you can shift your mindset and embrace the long-term benefits and security that saving provides.

Improving financial literacy and managing money effectively are the ultimate goals of this book, and developing a savings mindset is a crucial step toward achieving them. This subchapter will provide you with valuable insights into understanding the importance of saving, the power of compound interest, and various saving vehicles available to grow your wealth. It will also offer practical tips on how to track your progress, stay motivated, and make saving a lifelong habit.

In conclusion, developing a savings mindset is essential for anyone seeking financial freedom. By building healthy habits and routines, improving time management and organization skills, overcoming fear and phobias, and enhancing financial literacy, you can transform your relationship with money and pave the way for a secure and prosperous future. This subchapter will empower you with the knowledge, tools, and motivation to embark on this transformative journey towards financial freedom.

Smart Spending Strategies

In today's fast-paced world, where money seems to slip through our fingers faster than we can earn it, it has become crucial to develop smart spending strategies. By adopting these strategies, you can take control of your finances, improve your financial literacy, and ultimately achieve the much-desired state of financial freedom. In this subchapter, we will explore some effective techniques and habits that will help you make wise financial decisions and manage your money more efficiently.

One of the key principles of smart spending is tracking your expenses. By keeping a record of every penny you spend, you gain a clear understanding of where your money is going. This awareness enables you to identify areas where you can cut back and save more effectively. Utilizing budgeting apps or spreadsheets can simplify this process and provide you with valuable insights into your spending patterns.

Another valuable strategy is differentiating between needs and wants. Ask yourself whether a purchase is essential or simply a desire. By prioritizing your needs and consciously limiting your wants, you can avoid impulsive spending and save more for your financial goals. Additionally, taking the time to research and compare prices before making a purchase can help you find the best deals and avoid overspending.

Creating a personal finance plan is another crucial aspect of smart spending. Set specific financial goals and outline the steps needed to achieve them. Whether it's saving for a down payment on a house or paying off debt, having a clear plan will keep you motivated and focused on your objectives. Consider automating your savings and investments, as this reduces the temptation to spend money that should be saved or invested.

Furthermore, adopting a minimalist mindset can significantly impact your spending habits. By embracing a less-is-more philosophy, you can reduce clutter and unnecessary expenses, while also freeing up mental space and reducing stress. Simplifying your life not only saves you money but also enables you to appreciate the things that truly matter.

Lastly, it's important to regularly reassess your spending habits and make adjustments as needed. As your financial situation evolves, so should your spending strategies. Stay informed about new financial tools, investment opportunities, and money-saving techniques. By continuously educating yourself in the realm of financial literacy, you will be better equipped to make informed decisions and secure your financial future.

In conclusion, by implementing smart spending strategies, you can take control of your finances and work towards achieving financial freedom.

Automating Bill Payments and Savings

Whether it's tracking your expenses, differentiating between needs and wants, creating a personal finance plan, adopting a minimalist mindset, or staying informed about financial trends, each step you take brings you closer to your goals. Remember, financial freedom is not an overnight achievement but a journey that requires consistent effort and discipline. Start today and pave the way for a brighter financial future.

In today's fast-paced and busy world, managing our finances can often become a daunting task. Juggling multiple bills and ensuring timely payments can be overwhelming, not to mention trying to save money for future goals. However, there is a solution that can help alleviate some of these burdens - automating bill payments and savings.

Automating bill payments is a fantastic way to stay organized and avoid late fees or missed payments. By setting up automatic payments through your bank or credit card, you can ensure that your bills are paid on time, every time. No more scrambling to remember due dates or dealing with the stress of late payment penalties. With automated bill payments, you can have peace of mind, knowing that your financial responsibilities are taken care of effortlessly.

Another benefit of automating bill payments is the ability to track your expenses more efficiently. By reviewing your bank statements regularly, you can identify any unnecessary expenses and adjust your budget accordingly.

This practice will contribute to improving your financial literacy and managing your money more effectively.

In addition to bill payments, automating your savings is a powerful tool for building financial freedom. By setting up automatic transfers from your checking account to a savings or investment account, you are effectively making saving a priority. This habit will help you build a financial cushion for emergencies or work towards long-term goals, such as buying a house or retiring comfortably.

Automating your savings also helps in overcoming financial fears and phobias. It eliminates the need to manually transfer money, which can sometimes trigger anxiety or hesitation. By removing the decision-making process, you can establish a consistent savings routine without feeling overwhelmed or tempted to spend the money elsewhere.

Moreover, automating bill payments and savings extends beyond financial benefits. It helps improve time management and organization skills. With less time spent on manual payment transfers or worrying about missed due dates, you can focus on other important aspects of your life. This newfound time can be utilized to build healthy habits, reduce stress, and enhance overall well-being.

In conclusion, automating bill payments and savings is a key component of improving financial literacy and managing money effectively. By taking advantage of technology and setting up automated systems, you can save time, reduce stress, and build a healthier financial future. So why wait? Start automating your financial obligations today and take a step towards achieving financial freedom.

Establishing an Emergency Fund

In today's unpredictable world, having a solid financial foundation is essential for peace of mind and security. One crucial component of that foundation is establishing an emergency fund. This subchapter will guide you through the importance of having an emergency fund, how to set it up, and strategies to maintain and grow it.

An emergency fund serves as a safety net during unexpected life events such as job loss, medical emergencies, or major home repairs. It provides a financial cushion that allows you to handle these situations without resorting to credit cards or loans, which can lead to debt and financial stress.

To start building your emergency fund, determine how much you need to save. Financial experts recommend aiming for three to six months' worth of living expenses. Take into account factors such as your monthly bills, groceries, transportation costs, and any recurring payments. Calculate a realistic amount that will cover essential expenses should an emergency arise.

Next, devise a savings plan. Set aside a fixed amount from each paycheck to contribute to your emergency fund. Automating this process by creating an automatic transfer to your savings account will help ensure consistency and prevent the temptation to spend the money elsewhere.

Consider opening a separate savings account solely for your emergency fund. This separation creates a psychological barrier, making it less likely that you dip into the fund for non-emergency expenses. Additionally, choosing a high-yield savings account can help grow your emergency fund faster through accrued interest.

As you build your emergency fund, it's crucial to regularly reassess your financial situation to determine if adjustments are necessary. If your expenses increase or your income fluctuates, revisit your savings plan and make any modifications needed to maintain a healthy emergency fund.

Remember, emergencies can happen at any time. Stay committed to your savings plan, even when times are financially comfortable. Your emergency fund is your financial safety net, providing you with peace of mind and the ability to handle unexpected challenges without derailing your overall financial goals.

In conclusion, establishing an emergency fund is a critical step towards achieving financial freedom. By having a financial cushion, you'll be better equipped to handle any unexpected expenses that come your way. Make it a priority to set up and grow your emergency fund, and you'll be taking a significant step towards improving your financial literacy and managing money effectively.

Chapter 5: Improving Time Management for Financial Success

Prioritizing Financial Tasks

In our fast-paced world, it's easy to become overwhelmed with the constant demands on our time and energy. This is especially true when it comes to managing our finances. However, by prioritizing our financial tasks, we can take control of our money and ultimately achieve financial freedom.

One of the first steps in prioritizing your financial tasks is to create a budget. This is the foundation of your financial plan and will help you track your income and expenses. By having a clear understanding of where your money is going, you can make informed decisions about how to allocate your resources.

Next, it's important to establish an emergency fund. Life is full of unexpected expenses, such as medical bills or car repairs, and having a financial safety net can provide peace of mind. Aim to save at least three to six months' worth of living expenses in a separate, easily accessible account.

Debt management should also be a priority. High-interest debts, such as credit card balances, can quickly accumulate and hinder your financial progress. Make a plan to pay off these debts as soon as possible, focusing on the ones with the highest interest rates first. Consider consolidating your debts or negotiating with creditors to reduce interest rates or monthly payments.

Investing for the future is another essential financial task. Whether it's saving for retirement or building wealth, investing allows your money to work for you. Research different investment options, such as stocks, bonds, or real estate, and consider seeking advice from a financial advisor to help you make informed decisions.

Finally, don't forget to prioritize your financial education. Improving your financial literacy is an ongoing process that will empower you to make better financial decisions. Read books, take courses, or attend seminars to expand your knowledge and stay up to date with the latest trends and strategies in personal finance.

In conclusion, prioritizing your financial tasks is crucial for achieving financial freedom. By creating a budget, establishing an emergency fund, managing debt, investing for the future, and continuously improving your financial literacy, you'll be well on your way to building a solid financial foundation and managing your money effectively. Take control of your finances today and pave the way to a brighter financial future.

Creating a Daily and Weekly Financial Routine

In today's fast-paced world, it's easy to fall into the trap of neglecting our financial well-being. However, taking control of our finances is crucial for achieving financial freedom and peace of mind. To help you on this journey, it's essential to establish a daily and weekly financial routine. By doing so, you can build healthy habits, improve time management and organization skills, overcome fear and phobias related to money, and enhance your financial literacy and money management skills.

A daily financial routine involves setting aside a few minutes each day to review your financial transactions. This includes checking your bank accounts, credit card statements, and other financial statements. By monitoring your expenses and income regularly, you can identify any discrepancies or potential areas for improvement. It also helps you stay on track with your budget and savings goals.

Additionally, a daily routine should include allocating time for financial education. This can involve reading financial books, articles, or listening to podcasts that help you improve your financial literacy. By consistently educating yourself about personal finance, you'll gain valuable knowledge that can empower you to make better financial decisions.

On a weekly basis, it's important to set aside time to plan and organize your finances. This involves creating a budget for the upcoming week, reviewing your financial goals, and tracking your progress. By regularly evaluating your financial situation, you can make adjustments as needed and stay focused on your long-term financial objectives.

Furthermore, part of your weekly routine should involve setting financial goals for the upcoming week. These goals can be short-term targets that align with your long-term financial vision. Whether it's paying off a certain amount of debt, saving a specific percentage of your income, or investing in your retirement account, having these goals in mind will help you stay motivated and accountable.

By implementing a daily and weekly financial routine, you'll gradually develop healthy habits and improve your time management and organization skills. It will also help you overcome any fears or phobias related to money by taking proactive steps towards financial empowerment. Ultimately, this routine will enhance your financial literacy and money management skills, paving the way for long-lasting financial freedom and success.

Using Technology for Efficient Money Management

In today's fast-paced and technology-driven world, managing your finances can be made easier and more efficient with the help of various technological tools. Whether you are looking to build healthy financial habits, improve time management and organization skills, overcome fears and phobias related to money, or simply enhance your financial literacy, embracing technology can be a game-changer on your journey towards financial freedom.

One of the key benefits of using technology for money management is the ability to track your expenses in real-time. Gone are the days of manually recording every transaction in a checkbook register. With budgeting apps and online banking platforms, you can effortlessly categorize your expenses, set spending limits, and receive notifications when you are nearing your budget thresholds. This not only helps you stay on top of your finances but also enables you to identify areas where you may be overspending and make necessary adjustments.

Additionally, technology provides convenient access to financial education resources. There are countless online platforms, podcasts, and apps that offer valuable information on financial literacy and money management. These resources can help you learn about budgeting, investing, debt management, and other essential financial topics. By leveraging these tools, you can improve your understanding of personal finance and make informed decisions about your money.

For those who struggle with time management and organization, technology can offer effective solutions. With the help of digital calendars and reminder apps, you can set up recurring reminders for bill payments, track important financial deadlines, and stay organized with your financial tasks. This not only saves you time and reduces the chance of missing crucial financial obligations but also helps alleviate stress and anxiety associated with managing your money.

Moreover, technology can assist you in overcoming fears and phobias related to money. For instance, if you have a fear of investing, there are investment apps and robo-advisors that can guide you through the process and help you start investing with confidence. Similarly, if you are anxious about tracking your expenses, there are expense management apps that can automate the process and provide you with a clear overview of your spending habits.

In conclusion, incorporating technology into your money management practices can significantly improve your financial literacy and help you build healthy financial habits. By utilizing budgeting apps, online banking platforms, educational resources, and other technological tools, you can track your expenses, enhance your time management skills, overcome fears related to money, and ultimately achieve financial freedom. Embrace the power of technology and take control of your financial future today.

Delegating and Outsourcing Financial Responsibilities

In today's fast-paced world, where time is of the essence, finding ways to effectively manage our financial responsibilities can be a daunting task. However, by learning to delegate and outsource certain financial tasks, we can free up valuable time and energy to focus on what truly matters. This subchapter will explore the benefits of delegating and outsourcing financial responsibilities and provide practical tips on how to do so effectively.

One of the key reasons to delegate financial tasks is to build healthy habits and routines. By handing over certain responsibilities to trusted professionals or family members, we can develop a sense of accountability and discipline. This allows us to establish a consistent financial routine, ensuring that bills are paid on time, investments are monitored, and budgets are adhered to. Delegating also helps to alleviate stress and overwhelm, providing us with the mental space to make better financial decisions.

Improving time management and organization skills is another area where delegating and outsourcing can be highly beneficial. By offloading administrative tasks, such as bookkeeping, tax preparation, or bill payments, we can reclaim valuable hours in our day. This newfound time can then be spent on activities that truly align with our goals and values, whether it's pursuing a passion project, spending quality time with loved ones, or focusing on personal growth and self-care.

For those who struggle with fear and phobias around finances, delegating can serve as a powerful tool for overcoming these anxieties. By entrusting certain financial responsibilities to professionals who specialize in these areas, we can gain confidence and peace of mind. Whether it's seeking the guidance of a financial advisor, hiring an accountant, or utilizing software to automate certain tasks, delegating allows us to confront our fears head-on and gradually build financial literacy and resilience.

Lastly, delegating and outsourcing financial responsibilities can significantly improve our overall financial literacy and money management skills. By working with experts in various fields, we can tap into their knowledge and expertise, gaining insights that can help us make more informed decisions. Additionally, outsourcing tasks like investment analysis or retirement planning can help us navigate complex financial landscapes with greater ease and confidence.

In conclusion, delegating and outsourcing financial responsibilities can be a game-changer for individuals seeking to improve their financial literacy, manage their money effectively, build healthy habits, and overcome fears and phobias. By harnessing the power of delegation, we can create more time, reduce stress, and develop the necessary skills to take control of our financial future.

Chapter 6: Organizing Your Financial Life

Setting Up a Filing System for Financial Documents

In order to achieve financial freedom and effectively manage your money, it is crucial to have a well-organized filing system for your financial documents. This subchapter will guide you through the process of setting up a filing system that will enable you to easily access and manage your financial records.

1. Understand the Importance of Organizing Financial Documents: Managing your money requires keeping track of various financial documents such as bank statements, tax returns, insurance policies, and investment statements. By having a systematic filing system, you will be able to find the information you need quickly and avoid any unnecessary stress or confusion.

2. Gather the Necessary Supplies:

Before setting up your filing system, make sure you have the necessary supplies such as file folders, a filing cabinet or box, labels, and a label maker or pen. Having these supplies ready will make the process much smoother.

3. Categorize Your Financial Documents:

Start by creating categories for your financial documents. Some common categories include income, expenses, taxes, investments, insurance, and debt. Customize these categories based on your specific financial situation and needs.

4. Create a Logical File Structure:

Once you have your categories, create a logical file structure within each category. For example, under the expenses category, you can have subcategories like utilities, groceries, transportation, and so on. This will help you locate specific documents easily.

5. Label and Organize Your Files:

Label each file folder clearly with the appropriate category and subcategory. Use a label maker or a pen to ensure legibility. Place the files in the filing cabinet or box in a logical order, such as alphabetically or chronologically. This will make it easier to find specific documents when needed.

6. Regularly Maintain and Update Your Filing System:

Setting up a filing system is not a one-time task. It requires regular maintenance and updating. Set aside time every month or quarter to file new documents and review existing ones. Purge any outdated or unnecessary documents to keep your filing system clutter-free.

By following these steps and maintaining a well-organized filing system, you will have a solid foundation for managing your financial documents. This will not only save you time and effort but also provide you with peace of mind, knowing that your financial records are easily accessible and well-organized. Take control of your financial future by implementing this simple yet effective filing system.

Managing Digital Financial Records

In today's digital age, it is crucial to effectively manage our financial records to ensure financial stability and peace of mind. Gone are the days of keeping stacks of paper receipts and files. With the advancements in technology, we now have the convenience of digital financial records that can be easily accessed and organized. In this subchapter, we will explore the importance of managing digital financial records and provide practical tips to help you stay organized and make informed financial decisions.

One of the key benefits of digital financial records is the ability to access them anytime, anywhere. Whether you need to review past transactions, track expenses, or prepare for tax season, having your financial records digitized allows for easy retrieval and analysis. By implementing a system to manage your digital records, you can save time and effort in searching through physical documents.

To effectively manage your digital financial records, it is essential to establish a routine. Set aside specific time each week or month to organize and update your records. Create folders on your computer or cloud storage, categorizing expenses, income, and investments. Consider using software or apps that can automatically sync with your bank accounts and credit cards, simplifying the process of tracking and categorizing transactions.

Another important aspect of managing digital financial records is ensuring their security. Protecting your personal and financial information is paramount. Use strong passwords for your accounts and consider enabling two-factor authentication for added security. Regularly back up your digital records to an external hard drive or a secure cloud storage service. Be cautious when sharing sensitive information and only use secure websites for financial transactions.

In addition to organizing and securing your digital financial records, it is essential to maintain a clear and concise record-keeping system. Regularly review your records to identify any discrepancies or errors. Use software or spreadsheets to create personalized financial reports that can offer valuable insights into your spending habits and help you make informed financial decisions.

By effectively managing your digital financial records, you are taking a proactive step towards improving your financial literacy and managing your money. The convenience, accessibility, and security of digital records make it easier than ever to stay organized and in control of your finances. Implementing the tips mentioned in this subchapter will help you build healthy habits, improve time management and organization skills, overcome fears related to financial matters, and ultimately achieve financial freedom.

Simplifying and Optimizing Financial Accounts

In today's fast-paced and complex world, managing our finances can often feel overwhelming and confusing. However, taking control of our financial accounts is an essential step towards achieving true financial freedom. By simplifying and optimizing our financial accounts, we can improve our financial literacy, manage our money more effectively, and build healthy habits and routines that lead to a more organized and stress-free life.

One of the first steps towards simplifying our financial accounts is to consolidate them. Many of us have multiple bank accounts, credit cards, and investment accounts, which can make it difficult to keep track of our finances. By consolidating these accounts, we can streamline our financial management process and reduce the chances of missing important payments or transactions.

Another important aspect of optimizing our financial accounts is to automate our finances. Setting up automatic bill payments, savings transfers, and investment contributions can save us time and effort, while also ensuring that we never miss a payment or fail to save for our future. By automating our finances, we can focus on other important aspects of our lives, knowing that our financial responsibilities are being taken care of.

In addition to simplifying and automating our financial accounts, it is crucial to regularly review and update them. This involves monitoring our bank statements, credit card transactions, and investment portfolios to identify any errors or potential areas for improvement. By staying vigilant and proactive in managing our accounts, we can avoid unnecessary fees, maximize our returns, and minimize the risk of fraud or identity theft.

Furthermore, improving our financial literacy is key to optimizing our financial accounts. This includes educating ourselves about different financial products and services, understanding the basics of investing, and learning how to create and stick to a budget. By enhancing our financial knowledge, we can make informed decisions about our accounts and ensure that they align with our long-term financial goals.

Taking control of our financial accounts may seem daunting at first, but with the right mindset and strategies, it can become a rewarding and empowering process. By simplifying and optimizing our financial accounts, we can build healthy habits and routines, improve our time management and organization skills, overcome fears and phobias associated with money, and ultimately achieve true financial freedom. So, let's take the first step towards a brighter financial future by simplifying and optimizing our financial accounts today.

Reviewing and Updating Insurance Policies

Insurance is a vital component of a comprehensive financial plan. It provides protection against unexpected events and helps safeguard your financial well-being. However, simply purchasing insurance policies is not enough. Regularly reviewing and updating these policies is crucial to ensure they continue to meet your evolving needs and provide adequate coverage.

One of the first steps in reviewing your insurance policies is to assess any changes in your life or financial situation. Have you recently gotten married or divorced? Have you welcomed a new member to your family? Have you purchased a new home or vehicle? These life events can significantly impact your insurance needs, and it's essential to update your policies accordingly.

Another factor to consider when reviewing your insurance policies is changes in legislation and regulations. Insurance laws and regulations are constantly evolving, and it's important to stay informed about any updates that may affect your coverage. This is particularly relevant for health insurance policies, where changes in healthcare laws can impact your coverage options and costs.

Additionally, reviewing your policies allows you to assess the adequacy of your coverage limits. Over time, your financial situation may have improved, and you may need to increase your coverage to protect your assets adequately. On the other hand, if you have paid off debts or downsized your lifestyle, you may find that you can reduce coverage and save on premiums.

Furthermore, it's crucial to review the terms and conditions of your policies to understand any exclusions or limitations. This will help you determine if there are any gaps in your coverage that need to be addressed. For example, your homeowners' insurance policy may not cover certain natural disasters or valuable personal belongings, and you may need to add additional coverage to fill these gaps.

Regularly reviewing and updating your insurance policies is also an opportunity to shop around for better rates. Insurance premiums can vary significantly between providers, and comparing quotes can help you save money without compromising on coverage. However, it's important to ensure that you are comparing policies with similar coverage limits and deductibles to make an informed decision.

In conclusion, reviewing and updating insurance policies is a crucial aspect of financial management. It allows you to assess changes in your life and financial situation, stay informed about legislative updates, evaluate coverage adequacy, address any gaps in coverage, and potentially save money on premiums. By staying proactive with your insurance policies, you can ensure that you have the necessary protection to achieve financial freedom and peace of mind.

Chapter 7: Overcoming Fear and Phobias Related to Finances

Identifying and Addressing Money Anxiety

In today's fast-paced and ever-changing world, financial anxiety has become a common issue for many adults. The constant pressure to meet financial obligations, manage debts, and save for the future can create a sense of overwhelm and fear. However, it is important to recognize and address this money anxiety in order to achieve true financial freedom and improve overall well-being.

The first step in overcoming money anxiety is to identify its root causes. Take a moment to reflect on your financial situation and explore the emotions that arise when you think about money. Are you worried about not having enough to cover your expenses? Do you feel guilty or ashamed about past financial mistakes? By pinpointing the specific triggers of your anxiety, you can begin to develop strategies to address them.

One effective technique for managing money anxiety is to improve financial literacy. Educating yourself about personal finance will empower you to make informed decisions and regain a sense of control over your money. Start by reading books, attending workshops, or seeking guidance from financial professionals. Understanding concepts such as budgeting, investing, and debt management will help you build a solid foundation for financial success. Another important aspect of addressing money anxiety is developing healthy habits and routines. Effective time management and organization skills are crucial for maintaining financial stability. Create a realistic budget that aligns with your income and expenses, and stick to it. Establish a routine for tracking your spending, paying bills on time, and setting aside savings. By implementing these habits, you will experience a greater sense of financial security and reduce anxiety.

Overcoming fear and phobias associated with money is also essential for achieving financial freedom. Many individuals avoid dealing with financial matters due to fear of failure or making mistakes. To overcome this fear, start by setting small, achievable goals. Celebrate your successes along the way and learn from any setbacks. Surround yourself with a supportive network of friends or professionals who can provide guidance and encouragement.

By addressing money anxiety head-on, you can take control of your financial future and improve your overall well-being. Remember, financial freedom is not just about accumulating wealth, but also about finding peace of mind and security. By improving your financial literacy, developing healthy habits, overcoming fear and phobias, you can pave the way to a brighter and more prosperous future.

Confronting Financial Phobias and Overcoming Them

Introduction:

Financial phobias can be incredibly debilitating, causing immense stress and anxiety when it comes to managing one's money. These fears can prevent individuals from making sound financial decisions and hinder their path to financial freedom. In this subchapter, we will delve into the common financial phobias that plague many adults and provide practical strategies to overcome them. By addressing these fears head-on, we can pave the way for a healthier relationship with money and a more secure financial future.

Understanding Financial Phobias:

Financial phobias can manifest in various ways, such as fear of budgeting, investing, or dealing with debt. Many individuals are frightened by the mere thought of financial planning or making financial decisions, leading to avoidance and procrastination. It is crucial to recognize that these fears are normal but can be overcome with the right mindset and tools.

Overcoming Financial Phobias:

1. Educate Yourself: One of the most effective ways to conquer financial phobias is through financial literacy. By gaining knowledge about personal finance, budgeting, and investing, you can build confidence in making informed decisions. Seek out books, online resources, or even attend financial workshops to expand your financial knowledge.

2. Set Realistic Goals: Breaking down financial goals into smaller, achievable targets can help alleviate the overwhelming feeling associated with managing money. Start with simple goals, such as saving a specific amount each month, and gradually work your way towards more significant milestones.

3. Seek Professional Help: If your financial phobias are deeply rooted or causing significant distress, consider seeking help from a financial advisor or therapist specializing in financial anxiety. They can provide guidance, support, and strategies tailored to your specific needs.

4. Embrace Mindfulness and Positive Thinking: Practice mindfulness techniques to stay present and focused on your financial goals. Combat negative thoughts and fears by reframing them with positive affirmations. Remember that change takes time and effort, and setbacks are a natural part of the process.

Conclusion:

Confronting financial phobias is a crucial step towards achieving financial freedom. By understanding these fears, educating ourselves, setting realistic goals, seeking professional help when necessary, and embracing positive thinking, we can overcome financial phobias and regain control over our financial lives. Overcoming these fears will not only improve our financial literacy and money management skills but also contribute to building healthy habits and routines, improving time management, and overcoming other fears and phobias. Remember, it is never too late to confront your financial fears and pave the way towards a brighter and more secure financial future.

Seeking Professional Help and Support

In our journey towards financial freedom, it is essential to recognize that we cannot do it all on our own. Seeking professional help and support is a crucial step towards improving our financial literacy and managing money effectively. In this subchapter, we will explore the various avenues through which we can seek assistance in building healthy habits and routines, improving time management and organization skills, overcoming fear and phobias, and, above all, enhancing our financial literacy.

When it comes to building healthy habits and routines, a professional coach or mentor can provide valuable guidance. They can help us identify our goals, create a personalized plan, and hold us accountable for our actions. Whether it's creating a budget, saving for retirement, or developing a consistent savings habit, a professional can provide the expertise and motivation we need to stay on track.

Time management and organization skills are vital in our fast-paced and demanding lives. Seeking professional help in this area can ensure that we make the most of our time and prioritize tasks effectively. A professional organizer or time management coach can teach us practical techniques to streamline our routines, set realistic goals, and eliminate distractions. By mastering these skills, we can create a more balanced and productive life. Fear and phobias can sometimes hinder our progress, particularly when it comes to managing money. Whether it's a fear of investing, fear of debt, or fear of making financial decisions, seeking professional help can help us overcome these roadblocks. A therapist or financial counselor can help us understand the root causes of our fears, develop coping strategies, and build confidence in managing our finances. By addressing these fears head-on, we can regain control over our financial lives.

Lastly, improving our financial literacy requires continuous learning and education. Seeking professional help in this area can provide us with the necessary knowledge and skills to make informed financial decisions. Financial advisors or educators can guide us through complex concepts such as investing, tax planning, and retirement savings. They can also provide personalized advice based on our specific circumstances, helping us achieve our financial goals.

In conclusion, seeking professional help and support is an essential part of our journey towards financial freedom. Whether it's building healthy habits, improving time management, overcoming fears, or enhancing our financial literacy, professionals in these fields can provide valuable guidance and support. By recognizing the areas where we need assistance and seeking help, we can accelerate our progress and achieve long-term financial success. Remember, investing in ourselves is the best investment we can make.

Building Confidence in Financial Decision-Making

Financial decision-making can often be overwhelming and intimidating, especially if we lack the necessary knowledge and skills to navigate the complex world of money management. However, with the right tools and mindset, we can build confidence in making sound financial choices that will set us on the path to financial freedom. In this subchapter, we will explore practical strategies and techniques to help you strengthen your financial decision-making skills and improve your overall financial literacy.

One of the key factors in building confidence in financial decision-making is acquiring knowledge. Understanding the basics of personal finance, such as budgeting, saving, investing, and debt management, is essential. This knowledge will empower you to make informed choices and avoid common pitfalls. The book "Financial Freedom Blueprint" provides a step-by-step guide to improving financial literacy, offering clear explanations and practical examples to help you grasp the fundamentals.

Another aspect of building confidence in financial decision-making is developing healthy habits and routines. By implementing effective money management strategies, such as creating a budget, tracking expenses, and setting financial goals, you can establish a solid foundation for making informed choices. The book offers practical exercises and templates to help you create these habits and routines, ensuring you stay on track towards financial freedom.

Time management and organization skills are also crucial in building confidence in financial decision-making. Learning to prioritize tasks, manage deadlines, and stay organized with financial paperwork can significantly reduce stress and increase productivity. The book provides proven techniques and strategies for improving time management and organization skills, enabling you to focus on making sound financial decisions without feeling overwhelmed.

Overcoming fear and phobias related to money is another key aspect addressed in this subchapter. Understanding and addressing the underlying emotional barriers that may be hindering your financial decision-making is essential for building confidence. By exploring mindset shifts and adopting a positive attitude towards money, you can overcome fear and develop a healthier relationship with your finances. The book offers practical exercises and strategies to help you overcome these fears and phobias, empowering you to make confident financial choices.

In conclusion, building confidence in financial decision-making requires acquiring knowledge, developing healthy habits and routines, improving time management and organization skills, and overcoming fear and phobias related to money. The subchapter "Building Confidence in Financial Decision-Making" in the book "Financial Freedom Blueprint" provides a comprehensive guide tailored to adult readers seeking self-help in these areas. By following the step-by-step instructions and applying the practical strategies and techniques provided, readers can strengthen their financial decision-making skills and improve their overall financial literacy, ultimately leading them towards financial freedom.

Chapter 8: Navigating the World of Investments

Understanding Different Investment Options

In today's rapidly changing and uncertain financial landscape, it is crucial to have a solid understanding of different investment options. Whether you are a seasoned investor or someone just starting on their journey towards financial freedom, this subchapter will provide you with valuable insights into various investment avenues.

Investing can seem overwhelming, but with the right knowledge and guidance, it can be a powerful tool for building wealth and securing your financial future. This subchapter aims to simplify the complex world of investments and equip you with the necessary information to make informed decisions.

Firstly, we will explore traditional investment options such as stocks and bonds. Stocks represent ownership in a company and can provide potential growth and dividends, while bonds are fixed-income investments that offer regular interest payments. We will delve into the pros and cons of each and explain how to assess risk and potential returns.

Next, we will discuss real estate investment, an avenue that has proven to be a lucrative option for many. Real estate can provide both rental income and capital appreciation, making it an attractive long-term investment. We will explore different types of real estate investments, such as residential and commercial properties, and provide tips on how to evaluate potential opportunities.

Furthermore, this subchapter will shed light on alternative investment options such as mutual funds, exchange-traded funds (ETFs), and precious metals. These investments offer diversification and can help mitigate risk. We will explain the mechanics of each investment type and outline their potential benefits.

Moreover, we will touch upon the growing popularity of socially responsible investing and impact investing. These investment options allow individuals to align their financial goals with their values, making a positive impact on society and the environment.

Finally, we will emphasize the importance of diversification and asset allocation. A well-diversified portfolio can help reduce risk and increase the likelihood of achieving your financial goals. We will provide practical tips on how to allocate your investments across different asset classes based on your risk tolerance and financial objectives.

By understanding the various investment options available to you, you will be better equipped to make educated decisions that align with your financial goals. This subchapter will empower you to take control of your financial future and embark on a path towards financial freedom.

Diversifying Your Investment Portfolio

One of the key pillars for achieving financial freedom is to have a well-diversified investment portfolio. This subchapter will guide you through the importance of diversification and provide practical tips on how to achieve it. Diversification is the process of spreading your investments across various asset classes, industries, and geographical locations. By doing so, you reduce the risk associated with any single investment and increase your chances of earning consistent returns. This is because not all investments perform well at the same time, and some may even lose value. However, by diversifying, you can minimize the impact of poor-performing investments on your overall portfolio.

To begin diversifying your portfolio, start by investing in different asset classes. These can include stocks, bonds, real estate, commodities, and even alternative investments like cryptocurrencies. By allocating your money across a variety of asset classes, you can take advantage of different market conditions and reduce the risk of losing everything if one asset class underperforms.

Another important aspect of diversification is investing in different industries. For instance, if you have a significant portion of your portfolio invested in technology companies and the tech sector experiences a downturn, your entire portfolio could suffer. However, by allocating your investments across various industries such as healthcare, energy, or consumer goods, you reduce the impact of any single industry's performance on your overall returns. Geographical diversification is also crucial. Investing solely in your home country's stock market can expose you to risks associated with that specific economy. By investing in international markets, you can tap into the growth potential of different countries and protect your portfolio from unfavorable domestic economic conditions.

It's important to note that diversification does not guarantee profits or protect against losses, but it can significantly reduce risk. Regularly reviewing and rebalancing your portfolio is essential to ensure that your investments are still aligned with your financial goals and risk tolerance.

In conclusion, diversifying your investment portfolio is a critical step towards achieving financial freedom. By spreading your investments across various asset classes, industries, and geographical locations, you can minimize risk and increase your chances of consistent returns. Remember to regularly review and rebalance your portfolio to ensure it remains aligned with your goals. With a diversified portfolio, you can navigate the ups and downs of the market with confidence and improve your overall financial well-being.

Chapter 9: Planning for Retirement and Long-Term Financial Security

Evaluating Risk and Return

Evaluating risk and return is an essential step in making informed investment decisions. It involves assessing the potential risks associated with an investment and weighing them against the potential returns.

Here are some key factors to consider when evaluating risk and return:

1. Risk tolerance: Before making any investment, it is important to understand your risk tolerance. This refers to your ability to handle potential losses and the level of uncertainty you are comfortable with. Higher-risk investments may offer the potential for higher returns, but they also come with a higher chance of loss.

2. Investment horizon: The length of time you are willing to hold an investment can impact your risk and return. Generally, longer investment horizons allow for a higher tolerance for risk and potentially higher returns. Shorter investment horizons may require lower-risk investments to ensure the preservation of capital.

3. Diversification: Diversifying your investment portfolio is a risk management strategy. By spreading your investments across different asset classes, industries, and geographic regions, you can reduce the impact of any individual investment's poor performance. This can help mitigate risk while still seeking attractive returns.

4. Historical performance: Evaluating the historical performance of an investment can provide insight into its risk and return potential. While past performance does not guarantee future results, it can help identify trends and patterns that may influence investment decisions.

5. Fundamental analysis: Conducting fundamental analysis involves assessing the financial health, profitability, and growth prospects of a company or investment. This analysis can help identify risks and opportunities that may impact the potential return.

6. Market conditions: The overall market conditions can impact the risk and return of an investment. Factors such as economic indicators, interest rates, inflation, and geopolitical events can all influence investment outcomes. It is important to consider these external factors when evaluating risk and return.

7. Risk-adjusted return: It is crucial to consider the risk-adjusted return of an investment. This measure takes into account the level of risk associated with an investment and compares it to the potential return. Calculating risk-adjusted return helps investors assess whether the potential return is worth the level of risk taken.

In summary, evaluating risk and return involves assessing your risk tolerance, investment horizon, diversification, historical performance, fundamental analysis, market conditions, and risk-adjusted return. By considering these factors, you can make more informed investment decisions and manage your risk effectively.

Working with Financial Advisors and Investment Professionals

Working with financial advisors and investment professionals can be beneficial for individuals who want to grow their wealth, plan for retirement, or navigate complex financial markets. Here are some key points to consider when working with these professionals:

1. Determine your needs: Before seeking out a financial advisor or investment professional, identify your financial goals and needs. This will help you find an advisor who specializes in the areas that align with your objectives.

2. Credentials and qualifications: Look for professionals who have relevant certifications such as Certified Financial Planner (CFP), Chartered Financial Analyst (CFA), or Registered Investment Advisor

(RIA). These designations indicate that the advisor has met certain educational and ethical standards.

3. Fee structure: Understand how the financial advisor or investment professional is compensated. Some may charge a fee based on a percentage of assets under management (AUM), while others may charge an hourly fee or a flat fee. Make sure you are comfortable with the fee structure and understand any potential conflicts of interest.

4. Investment philosophy: Discuss the advisor's investment philosophy and approach. Are they focused on active or passive investing? Do they have a long-term perspective or a short-term trading strategy? Make sure their philosophy aligns with your risk tolerance and investment preferences.

5. Communication and accessibility: Find out how frequently the advisor will communicate with you and how accessible they are when you have questions or concerns. Clear and regular communication is crucial for a successful client-advisor relationship.

6. Track record and reviews: Research the advisor's track record and read client reviews or testimonials. Look for any disciplinary actions or complaints filed against them. This information can provide insights into their past performance and reputation.

1. Understand their role: Clarify the advisor's role in your financial journey. Are they solely providing investment advice, or will they also help with financial planning, tax optimization, estate planning, or other areas? Understand the scope of their services to ensure they can meet your comprehensive financial needs.

2. Trust and rapport: Building trust and rapport with your advisor is important. You should feel comfortable sharing personal and financial information with them. Seek out professionals who listen to your concerns, address your questions, and work collaboratively with you to achieve your financial goals.

Remember, working with financial advisors and investment professionals is a partnership, and finding the right fit for your needs is crucial. Take your time, do thorough research, and ask questions to ensure you make an informed decision.

Assessing Retirement Needs and Goals

Assessing retirement needs and goals is an important step in planning for a financially secure retirement. It involves evaluating various factors such as desired lifestyle, expected expenses, income sources, and potential financial risks. Here are some key steps to assess retirement needs and goals:

1. Determine desired lifestyle: Start by envisioning your ideal retirement lifestyle. Consider factors such as travel, hobbies, healthcare, and housing preferences. This will help you estimate the level of financial resources required to support your desired lifestyle.

2. Estimate retirement expenses: Calculate your expected retirement expenses by considering both essential and discretionary spending. Essential expenses include housing, healthcare, food, utilities, and transportation. Discretionary expenses include travel, entertainment, hobbies, and gifts. Make sure to account for inflation when estimating expenses.

3. Evaluate income sources: Assess your potential income sources in retirement. These may include pensions, Social Security benefits, retirement savings (such as 401(k) plans or IRAs), investments, and any other sources of income. Determine the expected amount and reliability of each income source.

4. Assess potential financial risks: Consider potential risks that could impact your retirement savings and income. These may include market volatility, healthcare costs, inflation, and longevity risk (the risk of outliving your savings). Evaluate strategies to mitigate these risks, such

as diversifying investments, purchasing long-term care insurance, and creating an emergency fund.

1. Calculate retirement savings needs: Based on your estimated expenses and income sources, calculate the amount of retirement savings required to achieve your goals. Consider using retirement calculators or consulting with a financial advisor to determine this amount.

1. Develop a retirement savings plan: Create a plan to save and invest for retirement based on your estimated savings needs. Determine the appropriate savings rate and contribution levels to meet your goals. Consider maximizing contributions to tax-advantaged retirement accounts, such as 401(k) plans or IRAs.

2. Monitor and adjust as needed: Regularly review your retirement plan to ensure it remains aligned with your goals and circumstances. Adjust your savings and investment strategies as necessary. Revisit your plan annually or whenever there are significant changes in your financial situation or retirement goals.

Remember that assessing retirement needs and goals is an ongoing process. It is important to regularly review and update your plan as your circumstances change to ensure that you stay on track towards a secure and comfortable retirement.

Exploring Retirement Account Options

There are several retirement account options available to individuals to help save for their future. Here are some of the most common options:

1. 401(k) Plan: This is an employer-sponsored retirement plan where employees can contribute a portion of their salary on a pre-tax basis. The contributions are invested in a range of investment options, and the

earnings grow tax-deferred until withdrawal. Some employers also offer a matching contribution, which is essentially free money.

2. Individual Retirement Account (IRA): This is a personal retirement account that individuals can open with a financial institution. There are two main types of IRAs: Traditional and Roth. With a Traditional IRA, contributions may be tax-deductible, and the earnings grow tax-deferred until withdrawal. With a Roth IRA, contributions are made with after-tax dollars, but qualified withdrawals in retirement are tax-free.

3. Simplified Employee Pension (SEP) IRA: This is a retirement plan for self-employed individuals or small business owners. Contributions are made by the employer on behalf of the employees, and these contributions are tax-deductible for the employer. Employees do not contribute directly to a SEP IRA.

   1. SIMPLE IRA: This retirement plan is designed for small businesses with 100 or fewer employees. Employees can contribute a portion of their salary on a pre-tax basis, and employers are required to make either matching contributions or non-elective contributions.

   2. Solo 401(k): This retirement plan is designed for self-employed individuals or small business owners with no employees, except for a spouse. It operates similar to a traditional 401(k) plan, but with additional features that allow for higher contribution limits.

When choosing a retirement account, it's important to consider factors such as the tax advantages, contribution limits, investment options, and any employer matching contributions. It's also a good idea to consult with a financial advisor to determine the best retirement account option based on your individual circumstances and goals.

Strategies for Maximizing Social Security Benefits

1. Delay claiming benefits: By waiting until your full retirement age or even until age 70, you can receive a higher monthly benefit amount. For each year you delay beyond your full retirement age, your benefit increases by a certain percentage, up to age 70.

2. Coordinate benefits with your spouse: If you are married, you may be eligible for spousal benefits based on your spouse's earnings record. Coordinating your claiming strategies with your spouse can help maximize your combined benefits.

3. Maximize your earning years: Social Security benefits are based on your highest 35 years of earnings. By working for a longer period of time or focusing on increasing your income during your peak earning years, you can potentially increase your benefit amount.

4. Consider the impact of early retirement: While you can start claiming Social Security benefits as early as age 62, doing so will result in a reduced monthly benefit amount. If possible, it may be beneficial to continue working and delay claiming benefits until your full retirement age or later.

5. Minimize taxable income: Social Security benefits may become taxable if your income exceeds certain thresholds. By strategically managing your other sources of income, such as retirement account withdrawals or part-time work, you can potentially minimize the amount of your Social Security benefits that are subject to taxation.

6. Review your earnings record: It's important to periodically review your Social Security earnings record to ensure its accuracy. Any errors or missing earnings could result in a lower benefit amount. You can review your earnings record online through your Social Security account or by contacting the Social Security Administration.

1. Understand the impact of working while receiving benefits: If you choose to work while receiving Social Security benefits before your full retirement age, your benefits may be reduced if your earnings exceed certain limits. However, these reductions are temporary and your benefit amount will be recalculated once you reach full retirement age.

2. Consider spousal and survivor benefits: If you are married or divorced, you may be eligible for spousal or survivor benefits based on your spouse's or ex-spouse's earnings record. Understanding the eligibility requirements and strategies for maximizing these benefits can help increase your overall Social Security income.

3. Consult with a financial advisor: Social Security claiming strategies can be complex and vary depending on individual circumstances. Working with a financial advisor who specializes in retirement planning can help you navigate the options and make informed decisions to maximize your Social Security benefits.

Estate Planning and Wealth Transfer

Estate planning and wealth transfer refer to the process of arranging for the orderly transfer of assets and wealth to the intended beneficiaries upon one's death. It involves creating a plan that outlines how assets will be distributed, minimizing taxes, and ensuring that the wishes of the deceased are carried out.

Estate planning typically involves the following components:

1. Will: A legal document that outlines how assets will be distributed after death. It also appoints an executor to handle the estate.

2. Trusts: Trusts are legal arrangements that hold assets for the benefit of beneficiaries. They can be used to minimize taxes, provide for minor children, or protect assets from creditors.

3. Power of Attorney: This document designates someone to make financial or healthcare decisions on behalf of the individual in case of incapacity.
4. Healthcare Directives: These documents outline an individual's wishes regarding medical treatment and end-of-life decisions.

Wealth transfer involves the actual transfer of assets to beneficiaries. This can be done through various methods, such as:

1. Probate: The legal process of validating a will and distributing assets according to its provisions. This process can be time-consuming and expensive.

1. Non-probate transfers: Certain assets, such as life insurance policies or retirement accounts, can be transferred directly to beneficiaries outside of probate
2. Gifting: Individuals can transfer assets during their lifetime through gifting strategies to reduce their taxable estate.

The goal of estate planning and wealth transfer is to ensure that assets are distributed according to the individual's wishes, minimize tax liabilities, and provide for the financial well-being of loved ones. It is important to consult with an estate planning attorney or financial advisor to create a comprehensive plan that meets individual needs and objectives.

Chapter 10: Protecting Your Financial Future

Understanding Insurance Coverage

Insurance coverage is a vital aspect of managing your finances and protecting yourself from unexpected events. In this subchapter, we will explore the basics of insurance and provide you with a comprehensive understanding of its importance in your financial journey.

Insurance is a contract between an individual and an insurance company, where the individual pays a premium in exchange for protection against potential financial losses. It acts as a safety net by transferring the risk of potential losses to the insurance company. Understanding the different types of insurance coverage available can help you make informed decisions when it comes to protecting your assets and loved ones.

One of the most common types of insurance coverage is health insurance. It provides financial protection against medical expenses and ensures access to quality healthcare. Understanding the terms and conditions of your health insurance policy, such as deductibles, co-pays, and network coverage, is essential to make the most of your coverage.

Auto insurance is another crucial type of coverage, especially if you own a vehicle. It protects you financially in case of accidents, theft, or damage to your vehicle. Understanding the different coverage options, such as liability, collision, and comprehensive coverage, can help you choose the right policy for your needs.

Homeowners or renters insurance is essential for protecting your property and belongings against theft, fire, or natural disasters. It provides coverage for both the structure and contents of your home. Understanding the policy limits, exclusions, and deductibles will help you ensure adequate coverage.

Life insurance is an important consideration, especially if you have dependents who rely on your income. It provides financial protection to your loved ones in the event of your death. Understanding the different types of life insurance, such as term life and whole life insurance, will help you choose the most suitable policy for your family's needs.

In addition to these common insurance types, there are various other specialized policies available, such as disability insurance, long-term care insurance, and umbrella insurance. Understanding these options and assessing your specific needs can help you build a comprehensive insurance portfolio. It is crucial to regularly review your insurance coverage and make adjustments as needed. As your life circumstances change, so do your insurance needs. By understanding the basics of insurance coverage and regularly evaluating your policies, you can ensure that you have adequate protection and peace of mind. Remember, insurance coverage is not just an expense but an investment in your financial security. It provides a safety net that allows you to navigate unexpected events without facing crippling financial burdens. By understanding insurance and making informed choices, you can build a strong foundation for financial freedom.

Safeguarding Against Identity Theft and Fraud

In today's digital age, where personal information is increasingly vulnerable to cybercrime, it is crucial to take proactive steps to protect ourselves against identity theft and fraud. This subchapter aims to provide you with essential knowledge and practical tips to safeguard your identity and financial well-being.

Identity theft occurs when someone wrongfully obtains your personal information, such as your social security number, bank account details, or credit card information, to commit fraudulent activities. The repercussions of identity theft can be devastating, leading to financial loss, damaged credit scores, and even legal troubles. However, by being proactive and vigilant, you can significantly reduce the risk of falling victim to identity theft.

One of the most effective ways to safeguard against identity theft is to monitor your financial accounts regularly. By reviewing your bank and credit card statements, you can identify any unauthorized transactions promptly.

Additionally, consider enrolling in credit monitoring services that can alert you to any suspicious activities or changes in your credit report.

Another crucial step is to create strong and unique passwords for all your online accounts. Avoid using common passwords or ones that include personal information, such as your date of birth or your pet's name. Instead, use a combination of uppercase and lowercase letters, numbers, and special characters. It is also recommended to regularly update your passwords and enable two-factor authentication whenever possible.

Phishing scams are another common tactic used by fraudsters to obtain personal information. Be cautious of emails or messages that appear to be from reputable sources but ask for sensitive information. Legitimate organizations will never ask you to provide personal details via email. If you receive such a request, contact the organization directly to verify its authenticity.

Lastly, it is essential to protect your physical documents and shred any sensitive information before disposing of it. This includes old bank statements, credit card offers, and any documents containing personal information. Investing in a cross-cut shredder can help ensure that your information remains secure.

By implementing these practices and staying informed about the latest scams and fraud techniques, you can significantly reduce the risk of identity theft and fraud. Remember, safeguarding your financial well-being is a continuous process that requires diligence and awareness. By taking control of your personal information, you can enjoy peace of mind and financial freedom.

Creating a Financial Safety Net

In today's unpredictable world, it is crucial to have a solid financial safety net to protect ourselves and our loved ones from unexpected emergencies and uncertainties. Building this safety net is an essential step towards achieving financial freedom and peace of mind. In this subchapter, we will explore the necessary strategies and habits that can help you create a robust financial safety net.

First and foremost, it is important to establish an emergency fund. This fund should ideally cover a minimum of three to six months' worth of living expenses. By setting aside a portion of your income each month, you can gradually build this fund over time. Having an emergency fund ensures that you have a cushion to fall back on during unforeseen circumstances such as job loss, medical emergencies, or unexpected repairs.

In addition to an emergency fund, it is equally important to have appropriate insurance coverage. This includes health insurance, life insurance, disability insurance, and homeowner's/renter's insurance. Insurance acts as a safety net by providing financial protection against potential risks and liabilities. It is essential to review your insurance policies periodically to ensure that they adequately cover your needs.

Another crucial aspect of creating a financial safety net is minimizing debt. High-interest debts can quickly drain your resources and hinder your ability to save. Developing a debt repayment plan and committing to it will not only alleviate financial stress but also free up funds to allocate towards your emergency fund and other savings.

Diversifying your income sources is another effective way to strengthen your financial safety net. Relying solely on a single source of income can be risky. By exploring multiple income streams such as investments, side hustles, or freelance work, you can enhance your financial stability and increase your overall earning potential.

Lastly, it is essential to continually educate yourself about personal finance and investment strategies. Improving your financial literacy can help you make informed decisions and navigate through various financial challenges. There are numerous resources available, including books, podcasts, and online courses, that can assist you in improving your financial knowledge.

By implementing these strategies and habits, you can create a robust financial safety net that will protect you during challenging times and allow you to confidently pursue your financial goals. Remember, building a safety net requires patience and consistency, but the peace of mind it provides is invaluable. Take control of your financial future today and start creating your own financial safety net.

Continual Learning and Staying Up-to-Date with Financial Trends

In today's rapidly changing financial landscape, it is crucial to stay updated with the latest trends and developments. The world of finance is constantly evolving, and to achieve financial freedom, it is essential to have a solid understanding of the current financial trends. This subchapter aims to equip you with the necessary knowledge and tools to stay ahead of the curve and make informed financial decisions.

The key to staying up-to-date with financial trends is continual learning. As an adult, it is imperative to embrace a lifelong learning mindset. Committing to ongoing education in the realm of finance will not only help you improve your financial literacy but also empower you to make sound financial choices. By staying informed about the latest trends, you can adapt your strategies accordingly and capitalize on emerging opportunities.

One way to continually learn and stay updated is by reading reputable financial publications, attending seminars, and participating in webinars hosted by industry experts. These resources provide valuable insights into the current financial landscape, covering topics such as investment strategies, market trends, and personal finance management. By regularly engaging with such resources, you can expand your knowledge and gain a competitive edge.

Another effective way to stay up-to-date is by joining online financial communities and forums. These platforms offer a space for like-minded individuals to discuss financial topics, share experiences, and exchange ideas. By actively participating in these communities, you can tap into a wealth of collective knowledge, stay informed about the latest trends, and gain valuable perspectives from other members.

Utilizing technology is also crucial in staying up-to-date with financial trends. With the advent of mobile applications and finance-related websites, accessing real-time information has become easier than ever. By leveraging these tools, you can monitor market fluctuations, track your investments, and receive timely updates on financial news. This technological integration empowers you to make informed decisions promptly.

Continual learning and staying up-to-date with financial trends play a pivotal role in improving your financial literacy and managing money effectively. By dedicating time and effort to stay informed, you can navigate the complex financial landscape with confidence and make informed decisions that align with your financial goals. Remember, knowledge is power, and in the world of finance, staying ahead is the key to achieving financial freedom.

Chapter 11: Sustaining Financial Freedom

Reviewing and Revising Financial Goals

In the pursuit of financial freedom, it is essential to periodically review and revise your financial goals. Financial goals act as guiding principles that help you make informed decisions about money management and provide a clear path to achieving financial success. This subchapter will explore the importance of reviewing and revising financial goals and provide practical strategies to ensure your goals remain relevant and achievable.

Reviewing your financial goals is crucial because life is constantly changing, and so are your priorities. What may have been a significant financial goal a year ago may no longer hold the same importance today. By regularly reviewing your goals, you can adjust them to align with your current circumstances and aspirations. This process allows you to stay motivated and focused on what truly matters to you.

To begin the review process, take a step back and reflect on your current financial situation. Assess your income, expenses, debt, and savings. Analyze your progress towards your existing goals and evaluate whether they are still realistic and attainable. Consider any life changes, such as a new job, marriage, or starting a family, that may influence your financial goals.

Once you have evaluated your current financial standing, it is time to revise your goals. Start by setting specific, measurable, achievable, relevant, and time-bound (SMART) goals. Break down your long-term objectives into smaller short-term goals to make them more manageable and trackable. Assign deadlines to each goal to maintain accountability.

Additionally, consider seeking professional advice from a financial planner or advisor. They can provide valuable insights and help you create a realistic roadmap to achieving your financial goals. Their expertise can also assist you in identifying potential obstacles and developing strategies to overcome them.

Lastly, remember that reviewing and revising financial goals is an ongoing process. Life is unpredictable, and circumstances change. Regularly assess your progress, make necessary adjustments, and celebrate your achievements along the way. By continuously reviewing and revising your financial goals, you will ensure that you are on the right path towards financial freedom.

In conclusion, reviewing and revising financial goals is a vital step in your journey towards financial freedom. By regularly assessing your goals, making necessary adjustments, and seeking professional advice, you can stay motivated and focused on achieving your financial aspirations. Remember, financial goals are not set in stone; they are meant to evolve with you as you progress through life. So take the time to review, revise, and stay committed to your financial goals, and watch as your financial future transforms before your eyes.

Celebrating Milestones and Progress

Subchapter: Celebrating Milestones and Progress

Introduction:

In our journey towards financial freedom, it is crucial to acknowledge and celebrate the milestones and progress we make along the way. Often, we get so caught up in the pursuit of our goals that we forget to appreciate how far we have come. This subchapter will explore the significance of celebrating milestones and progress, and how it can contribute to our overall well-being and success.

Acknowledging Small Victories:

In our quest for financial literacy and managing money, it is important to recognize the small victories that occur daily. Whether it is successfully sticking to a budget, paying off a debt, or consistently saving a percentage of our income, these accomplishments deserve recognition. By acknowledging these small victories, we reinforce positive habits and build our confidence, motivating us to continue on our path towards financial freedom.

Motivation and Momentum:

Celebrating milestones and progress plays a vital role in maintaining our motivation and momentum. As we set and achieve short-term goals, we experience a sense of accomplishment and fulfillment. Celebrating these milestones not only boosts our self-esteem but also provides the necessary motivation to tackle bigger challenges. By breaking down our financial journey into manageable milestones, we create a roadmap that keeps us focused and determined.

Overcoming Fear and Phobias:

For many individuals, fear and phobias are significant barriers to financial success. Whether it is the fear of investing, the fear of addressing debt, or the fear of failure, these emotions can hinder progress. Celebrating milestones and progress helps us confront and overcome these fears. Each milestone achieved serves as evidence that we are capable of overcoming financial obstacles, instilling a sense of courage and resilience within us.

Building Healthy Habits and Routines:

Celebrating milestones and progress also reinforces healthy habits and routines. Consistently practicing good financial habits, such as budgeting, saving, and investing, can be challenging. By celebrating the progress made towards these habits, we reinforce their importance in our lives. This positive reinforcement encourages us to continue making healthy financial choices, ultimately leading to long-term success.

Conclusion:

In our pursuit of financial freedom, celebrating milestones and progress is not just a luxury; it is a necessity. By acknowledging our achievements, we reinforce positive habits, maintain motivation, overcome fears, and build a solid foundation for financial success. So, take a moment to reflect on how far you have come and celebrate your milestones – no matter how small – because each step brings you closer to the financial freedom you desire.

Teaching Financial Literacy to Others

Financial literacy is a crucial life skill that many adults struggle with. It involves understanding how money works, managing personal finances effectively, and making informed financial decisions. In today's complex financial landscape, it is more important than ever to equip ourselves with the knowledge and skills to achieve financial freedom. However, it is equally important to spread this knowledge and empower others to take control of their financial lives.

This subchapter delves into the art of teaching financial literacy to others. Whether you want to educate your family members, friends, or even organize workshops for your community, this section provides valuable insights and practical strategies to effectively convey financial concepts and principles.

One of the key aspects of teaching financial literacy is to understand the needs and aspirations of your audience. As adults, we have various niches we can tap into, such as self-help for building healthy habits and routines, improving time management and organization skills, overcoming fear and phobias, and of course, improving financial literacy and managing money. Recognizing these niches will help tailor your teaching approach and make the content more relevant and engaging.

To teach financial literacy effectively, it is important to simplify complex financial concepts. Break down jargon and explain terms in a way that is easy to understand. Use relatable examples and real-life scenarios to demonstrate the practical implications of financial decisions. Moreover, encourage active participation by incorporating interactive exercises and discussions that encourage critical thinking and problem-solving.

Another crucial aspect of teaching financial literacy is addressing the psychological barriers that often hinder individuals from taking control of their finances. Many people have deep-rooted fears and phobias associated with money, such as the fear of budgeting, fear of investing, or fear of financial failure. By acknowledging and addressing these fears, you can create a safe and supportive environment that empowers individuals to overcome their financial anxieties.

Furthermore, teaching financial literacy should focus not only on theory but also on practical application. Provide practical tools and resources that individuals can use to improve their financial situation. Teach them how to create a budget, save effectively, and invest wisely. By giving them the tools they need, you enable them to take immediate action and witness the positive impact on their financial well-being.

In conclusion, teaching financial literacy to others is a noble and impactful endeavor. By tailoring your teaching approach to the needs and niches of your audience, simplifying complex concepts, addressing psychological barriers, and providing practical tools, you can empower individuals to take control of their financial lives and achieve true financial freedom.

Giving Back and Contributing to Financial Education Initiatives

One of the most empowering actions you can take on your journey towards financial freedom is giving back and contributing to financial education initiatives. By sharing your knowledge and experiences, you not only assist others in improving their financial literacy but also reinforce and deepen your own understanding of the subject matter. This subchapter will explore various ways you can contribute to these initiatives and make a positive impact on the lives of others.

Firstly, consider volunteering your time and expertise at local schools, community centers, or non-profit organizations that focus on financial education. Many adults and young people lack the basic knowledge necessary to make informed financial decisions, and by offering your insights and guidance, you can help bridge this gap. Whether it's conducting workshops, giving presentations, or simply mentoring individuals, your contribution can have a lasting impact on their financial well-being.

Another way to contribute is by creating and sharing educational content. With the advent of the internet and social media, it has never been easier to reach a wide audience with your knowledge and advice. Start a blog, create videos or podcasts, or even write articles for reputable financial websites. By consistently producing valuable content, you can reach individuals who may not have access to traditional financial education resources.

Furthermore, consider partnering with local organizations or financial institutions to develop and deliver financial education programs. By combining your expertise with their resources, you can create impactful initiatives that reach a larger audience. This could involve teaching budgeting skills, explaining the importance of saving and investing, or helping individuals navigate complex financial systems.

Lastly, consider supporting financial education initiatives financially. Many non-profit organizations rely on donations to continue their important work.

By contributing financially, you are directly supporting the development and implementation of programs that improve financial literacy. This can be done through one-time donations or by setting up a recurring contribution to ensure sustained support.

Giving back and contributing to financial education initiatives not only benefits others but also contributes to your own growth and understanding of financial literacy. By sharing your knowledge, volunteering your time, creating educational content, partnering with organizations, or supporting initiatives financially, you can help create a more financially literate society and empower individuals to take control of their financial futures.